HOME SERIES

HOME SERIES
DINING ROOMS

BETA-PLUS

CONTENTS

P. 4-5
The sober and robust Aga fits very well in this kitchen created by Francis Van Damme. The dining room and chimney *lambris* are by Bart Speck.

P. 6
A long Island atmosphere in this dining room created by Fabienne Dupont and Alexander Cambron. Architecture: Hans Demyttenaere.

INTRODUCTION

K itchen and dining room are the true gathering places in most households.

Cooking, eating, discussing, ... bring a family together every day and are frequently the centerpiece for gathering with friends.

The formal dining rooms of yesteryear have given way to the convivial rooms we know today. Nowadays, the dining room is a place where the whole family can come together, which is often integrated into a large open kitchen, and sometimes accommodated in an adjoining room.

This new book features hundreds of lavish, inspirational images for planning and designing your new dining room.

P. 8
A dining room designed by Stéphanie Laporte (The Office).

P. 10-11
A Themenos project. The kitchen work surface in Statuario marble is by Van den Weghe (The Stonecompany). The flagstones on the floor are by Rik Storms.

A BALANCE BETWEEN

FUNCTIONALITY AND AESTHETICS

D oran for Country Cooking builds complete interiors in a streamlined or country style, placing the kitchen and the dining area at the centre of the design concept. Traditional craftsmanship is always an essential element of these designs.

The company creates customised solutions for every aspect of life at home.

A balance between functionality and aesthetics is the key to a successful interior design.

The distinctive dining area in this report is a fine example of the company's philosophy, which results in a unique atmosphere.

A kitchen with a Godin stove. Furniture in solid wood, with work surfaces in Belgian bluestone.
Traditional wall tiles from the Doran collection. Floor tiles in natural stone from Doran's Fleur de Lys collection.

The grand orangery creates a harmonious connection between the living room and the kitchen.

HARMONY IN BLACK, WHITE

AND BLEACHED WOOD

De Menagerie is a company specialising in the design and creation of custom-built kitchens and dining areas.

These designs are created on the basis of close consultation with the clients.

Key to their approach is the aim for balance and the synthesis of the architectural space with functionality and aesthetics to create a unique whole.

These kitchens are completely built by hand, using traditional techniques, with the focus on the high quality of the materials and finish.

This results in a very personal look that harmonises beautifully with the atmosphere of the house and the lifestyle of the owners.

This philosophy for living is perfectly illustrated by this project.

The arrangement of white and black blocks and the beautiful light lends a meditative atmosphere to this room in a polder house by the coast. Simplicity and calm set the tone.
The Aga stove and the raised fireplace make this a very cosy home.
The MDF drawers and doors have no handles and have been given a white paint finish.
Work surface in solid 5 cm-thick bluestone, with a rounded edge.

TIMELESS DINING

IN A SEASIDE APARTMENT

F or many years, Alain and Brigitte Garnier have combined their work as antiques dealers with a passion for design, creating timeless interiors suffused with elegance and sophistication.

For this tiny ground-floor apartment in Duinbergen (on the Belgian coast near Knokke), Garnier selected a number of distinctive antiques that were a perfect match for the robust, natural materials and linen curtains.

P. 21-23
The open kitchen and dining area sets the tone: untreated oak for the floors and units, in harmony with Belgian bluestone. The stove is by Lacanche.

OPEN AND SPACIOUS

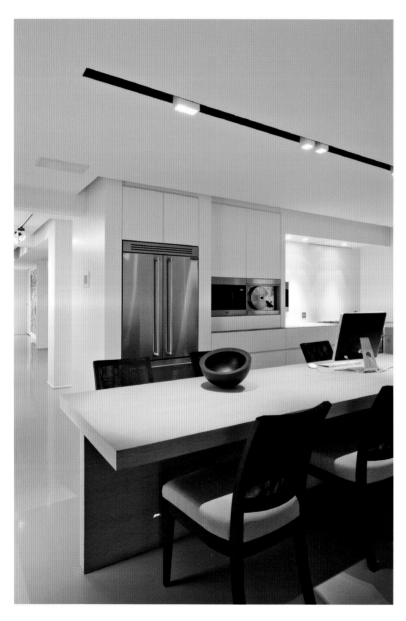

I nterior architect Dennis T'Jampens transformed an old factory space of 200 m^2 to a timeless, open and spacious loft.

The home exudes restraint and unity: straight lines, symmetrical structure, a combination of warm, lavish materials like oak and weathered marble and the white lacquered joinery ensure balance and calm.

P. 25-27
The Kreon lighting perfectly suits the house style of Dennis T'Jampens and gives the home an exclusive touch.
A central fireplace (De Puydt) offers a view from the dining to the living area.

A PASSION FOR WOOD

In less than two decades, Corvelyn have made a name for themselves as the wood specialist for renowned architects, interior designers and private clients.

This family company manufactures wooden floors in new and old woods, such as oak, pitch pine, elm, teak and more exotic varieties.

An expert in antique construction materials, Jan Corvelyn also goes out in search of unusual lots of wood, for instance wide boards in an exotic wood from Sri Lanka, an antique wooden floor from a Bulgarian barracks, broad pine planks from granaries in the Jura, brushed boards from a warehouse in Nancy, antique wooden stairs from Fontainebleau, ...

The dining room in a villa designed by architect Stéphane Boens. The old oak planks have been bleached.

P. 29-31

An authentic Zen atmosphere in this kitchen and dining area finished with reclaimed exotic planks that have been exposed to the sun, the sea, the wind and the rain for many years.

A MINIMALIST FARMHOUSE

T his 19th-century farmhouse has been freshened up and given an more contemporary feel.

Original elements were retained as far as possible, and nothing about the existing structure of the house was changed: a gentle renovation.

The breakfast room, with chairs by
Maxalto in white linen.
Two works of art by Paul Trajman.
Narrow console with a lamp, both by
Liaigre.

P. 34-35

The floor of the kitchen and dining area is in Pietra di Medici slabs (120x80 cm). The original beams have been whitewashed. Elm table and chairs (covered with Libeco linen) from am projects. Wooden block and lamp by Liaigre. Lighting in the beams by Mexcal (from Kurve).
The kitchen was created by Obumex, partly in white-painted MDF, partly in bleached oak.

CREATIVITY AND CRAFTSMANSHIP

F ahrenheit is the cooking shop par excellence. The company designs kitchens and distributes stoves and other professional and semi-professional kitchen equipment.

Owner Thierry Goffin has developed a unique concept of "culinary ergonomics": the kitchen is not simply a nice space, but is a real "living room", where cooking is an absolute pleasure. Top professionals ensure the design of the perfect kitchen / dining area, built in the best of materials and equipped with appliances of the highest standard.

In this eighteenth-century farmhouse, the traditional dining room has been replaced by a space with a long table / cooking island, where the cook can prepare a meal as friends and family members look on.
Ten people can sit comfortably around this majestic table in Belgian walnut wood.

P. 40-43
Kitchen and dining room form a whole beneath this authentic 18th-century beam, with a large sitting room and open fireplace behind. Thierry Goffin worked with a craftsman from Liège to create a padded barstool to match the height of the island. The finish of the stools shows the unparalleled classic elegance of this furniture.

REFURBISHMENT

OF A 1920'S HOUSE

Many years were required to give this home from the 1920's a timeless, contemporary look.

Various principles were important: letting in light in all the spaces, creating a contemporary but more importantly a warm interior with the integration of uncommon materials, and creating a well designed chaos to give this realisation a dramatic look. Design by Ensemble & Associés.

CH24 chairs by Hans Wegner in soaped beech around a table by Carl Hansen. Cubrik hanging light by Santa & Cole.

A Bulthaup kitchen with glossy varnish, black composite stone and walnut. The floor is covered with granito. The window along the work surface allows the nature to "enter" the kitchen.

AN OPEN SENSE OF SPACE

This wonderfully located penthouse was designed by Filip Glorieux and his team as the main residence for an active family.

The task consisted of connecting three apartments into a single residential whole with different functions that fulfil the wishes of the occupants.

Filip Glorieux and his team realised the design, execution and coordination of this unique total project.

An open sense of space is created by using floor to ceiling sliding and turning doors, which allows one optimally to enjoy the breathtaking views. In their closed position these doors provide the necessary privacy and intimacy.

The open fireplace, between kitchen and sitting area, reinforces the open character of this apartment and the cosy atmosphere.

A central stair connects the bottom apartment (that functions as a reception area and office) and the top apartment with the private accomodation.

SPACE AND LIGHT

When this client decided to renovate his detached home in a village, the items at the top of his wishlist were space and light.

Daan Van Troyen (architect) and Koen Aerts (interior designer) incorporated the technical equipment, storage space, entrance hall and stairway within the existing building.

Daan Van Troyen created a large extension at the back of the house to ensure the desired amount of space in the kitchen, dining room and living room.

A dining area was created between the kitchen and the sitting room. The long table accentuates the length of this space. The splashes of red add a more playful touch to this streamlined interior.

The interior architects designed the kitchen, which was then constructed by Decoeyer/decoform. The units are partly in aged oak and partly in a matte satin finish. The surfaces are in brushed stainless steel.

A CONTEMPORARY VILLAGE HOME

This small village home, nestled in the heart of the Gaume region, was removed completely to house a young family.

The resolutely contemporary interior, in contrast with the authentic character of the facades, was rethought to maximise the space by Ensemble & Associés.

There is a view of everything from the kitchen ... the living room, the dining room and the family room, all designed in neutral, soft shades.

A house where it is pleasant to spend time, surrounded by beautiful nature.

The kitchen was designed by Ensemble & Associés and finished in sandblasted, bleached oak and Crema composite stone. Taps by Dornbracht.

P. 60-61
The library is also a design by Ensemble & Associés, realised in sandblasted and bleached oak. CH24 chairs by Hans Wegner and a table by Carl Hansen.

A TIMELESS COUNTRY HOUSE

V lassak-Verhulst, the exclusive villa construction company, built this stately country house with a number of outbuildings. The house, situated in magnificent surroundings near Bergen aan Zee (Dutch coast), was then handed over to Sphere Concepts, designers and creators of the interior of this timeless country house.

The kitchen with a corner hearth and easy chair. Floors in Buxy cendré (120x70 cm).

The cooking area with a stainless-steel cooker and a work surface in composite stone.

P. 64-65
A table in reclaimed oak and custom-made lampshades in plissé linen.

TIMELESS, PRACTICAL

AND LOW ENERGY

T he design of this low energy home, created by the architect Annik Dierckx, is timeless and practical. The newest materials and most recent technologies were used.

The living spaces on the ground floor are arranged along a broad, central circulation axis that offers the possibility of allowing the spaces to flow into each other by opening the sliding partitions.

The large, atmospheric living kitchen perfectly suits the needs of contemporary, hectic life: cooking, dining, playing, entertaining guests, …

The rigid total design by the hand of a single architect, who designed both the interior and the exterior of the home, exudes warmth and harmony.

Light and fire are constantly recurring elements in the home, around which the living kitchen and lounge areas are constructed.

A LIGHT AND OPEN HOLIDAY HOME

An apartment from the 1980's was converted by the interior architect Philip Simoen into a light and open holiday home.

Lava rock from Dominique Desimpel was chosen as floor covering.

P. 72-77
All the custom made furniture was realised by D Interieur, the freestanding furniture (including an MDF table, Arper chairs, B&B sofas, Breuer Chair, Bertoia barstools, ...) is from Loft Living.
A fireplace realised by the company Pauwels, lighting from Modular.
The kitchen work surface was realised in Corian marble.

DEDICATED TO HARMONY

A haven of tranquillity set at the heart of a 6-hectare park on the outskirts of Brussels: the countryside at the town's doorstep. Transformed by the architects A.R.P.E. (Antoine de Radiguès) and the general construction firm Macors, this small, resolutely New England-style manor house is dedicated to harmony.

With noble materials, large rooms, daring decorative creations from Lionel Jadot and green spaces completely redesigned by Michel Delvosalle ... the constant interaction between the house and the surrounding natural environment is clear for all to see.

The kitchen and its imposing Aga cooker are located next to the dining area.

P. 80-81
The impressive dining room is separated
from the kitchen by a partition made from
glass and wrought iron.

COUNTRY STYLE

IN BLACK AND WHITE

F or this home, created by architect Gregory Dellicour for Mi Casa, the challenge was to reconcile a wooden structure with a contemporary interior.

Ensemble & Associés realised a successful project: when you enter this home, you are overwhelmed by a true holiday feel.

A table by Christian Liaigre and CH24 chairs designed by Hans Wegner. Photography by Franck Christen.

P. 86-89
The kitchen was entirely designed by Ensemble & Associés and realised in sandblasted oak. The composite stone work surface has been bevelled to 45°.

DINING IN IDYLLIC COUNTRYSIDE

This old farmhouse, situated in the green outskirts of Antwerp on a castle estate, has recently been completely restored by AIDarchitects (G. Van Zundert / K. Bakermans).

The house is in idyllic countryside, with a garden of several hectares that merges with the surrounding nature.

The restoration was kept as authentic as possible, with no superfluous adornment: the aim was to create a calm living environment for a young, dynamic family, with a focus on functionality and space.

The use of old, natural materials in combination with some contemporary elements has also helped to create a special, distinctive feel in this home.

P. 92-93
Magnificent views of the garden combine with harmonious decor throughout the property.

A WARM ATMOSPHERE

With the conversion of a villa in Antwerp for a family with children the guiding principle for Cy Peys was to ensure the incidence of as much natural light as possible. She also strove for harmony by allowing various rooms to run into each other with new materials and by creating new entrances and proportions in the various rooms.

All the materials were used honestly and purely: a rigorous and consistent whole.

The warm atmosphere is emphasised by the dark oak floors and the wengé furniture.
The intimacy of the dining room is put in the limelight a little more through the use of raffia on the walls.

P. 96-97
White plastered walls make the spaces visually broader and more luminous. The uninterrupted sequence of all the functions is very clearly present in this villa: living, dining room and kitchen are all beautiful and well proportioned rooms that were connected harmoniously by Cy Peys.

CASA NERO

asa Nero refers to the name of the interior design agency of the owners (Casa Vero) and to the black brick volume that make up their home, designed by BBSC-Architects.

Closed on the roadside but completely open towards the broad meadow landscape at the back, which makes contact with nature optimal.

Open plan inside, a central rigid box in the middle that still provides some division without completely cutting off the contact between the areas.

The ground floor can be used flexibly; central kitchen, lounge and dining area and living room can be used together as larger rooms.

P. 102-105
The coarse, dark veneer and the white lacquer of the
furniture provide calm and unity. Everything is taut
but light and smooth contrast with dark and texture.

THE CHARM

OF ANTIQUE WOODEN PLANKS

ver the years, Corvelyn has built up an important collection of old wooden floors.

A tour of the company's spacious stockrooms is a revelation for most visitors: an 18th century antique oak parquet floor from Paris, old American pitch-pine planks up to 12m in length and 30 cm wide, antique cheesboards of over 4m in length and 30 cm wide, antique teak planks from Bali, wide pine attic planks from an old post office. Visitors with a love for old wood are sure to find something to please them.

Old oak planks have been used to great effect in this dining room. The timeworn look is the result of centuries of use.

THE BISTRO OF "CHEZ ODETTE"

A s a homage to the owner of a small bistro in the village, the property developer named her new hotel "Chez Odette", a charming guesthouse with six rooms and a refined kitchen.

The bistro of "Chez Odette" is one of the many rooms designed by Ensemble & Associés for this contemporary and trendy hotel.

The hotel bistro is a place where guests rediscover the pleasure of the countryside in a contemporary style.

CONTEMPORARY FEEL IN A SOUTH

OF FRANCE HOLIDAY HOME

Collection Privée is a renowned company in the world of home furnishings, with offices in Cannes and in Valbonne.

The company also has an architecture and an interior design conception firm, managed by Gilles Pellerin and Nicolette Schouten.

Flexform chairs around a dining table by Baltus. A bronze, "Forever" on the background. Sideboard and shelves from lacquered oak, also by Baltus. The light is by Ralph Lauren.

The Carube dining table is made from weathered oak. The chairs are covered in a linen case.

AN ELEGANT FINISHING TOUCH

T his dining room is representative for the very individual style of Filip Vanryckeghem (iXtra Interior Architecture): a combination of simple, streamlined design with warm, natural materials and colours.

The interior designer has introduced ebony as an accent on the fitted units, with black Corian as an elegant finishing touch. Chairs by B&B Italia (model: Metropolitan).

A FASHIONABLE LIVING

AND DINING KITCHEN

P aul van de Kooi's team designs and creates exclusive fitted kitchens to satisfy the most demanding of clients: connoisseurs of design and luxurious home comfort.

Over the years, Paul van de Kooi has become a familiar name in the Low Countries. His company guarantees top-quality kitchens that suit the client perfectly: from classic country kitchens to streamlined contemporary designs.

The work surfaces and sides of this Paul van de Kooi kitchen project were created with concrete poured on site. Interior cupboards were glued waterproof with birch multiplex, the three-layer oak fronts were finished in a graphite gray tint. Cooking plate from PITT Cooking and a Viking fridge.

HOME SERIES

Volume 21 : DINING ROOMS

The reports in this book are selected from the Beta-Plus collection of home-design books: www.betaplus.com
They have been compiled in a special series by Le Figaro in French language: Ma Déco

Copyright © 2010 Beta-Plus Publishing / Le Figaro
Originally published in French language

PUBLISHER
Beta-Plus Publishing
Termuninck 3
B – 7850 Enghien
Belgium
www.betaplus.com
info@betaplus.com

TEXT
Alexandra Druesne

PHOTOGRAPHY
Jo Pauwels

DESIGN
Polydem - Nathalie Binart

TRANSLATIONS
Txt-Ibis

ISBN : 978-90-8944-074-7

Printed in China

P.116-117
A dining room designed by Kultuz. The existing radiators were boxed in and painted in the colour of the walls.

P.118-119
An authentic Knoll table with marble surface and matching chairs in the dining room. A Daskal-Laperre project.

P.120-121
This dining room in a listed building has been designed by Yvette Feder

(Fedecor). Lighting study by Jozeph Zajfman.

P.122-123
Daring colour combinations in this ultramodern Paul van de Kooi kitchen. The fronts of the cupboard sides from MDF were sprayed in high gloss pink. The inside cupboards were glued waterproof in birch multiplex, the fronts of the island consist of three layers of oak with a whitewash finish. A Staron work surface.

P.124-125
La vie en rose, signed by Paul van de Kooi: birch laminate interiors and fronts in solid oak, with a pink gloss finish. The concrete work surface was cast in situ. Stove and fridge-freezer by Viking.

P.126-127
A Minus project: the living room, dining area, kitchen and storage were designed as a single open space.